Draft
Environmental Assessment and
Interim Comprehensive Conservation Plan

I0435086

For Establishment
of the
Lost Mound National Wildlife Refuge

Carroll and Jo Daviess Counties,
Illinois

September 2001
Prepared by:
U.S. Department of the Interior
Fish and Wildlife Service
Great Lakes-Big Rivers Region
Twin Cities, Minnesota

Contents

Figures

Interim Comprehensive Conservation Plan

Interim Compatibility Determination

Draft Environmental Assessment for Establishment of the Lost Mound National Wildlife Refuge in Northwestern Illinois

INTRODUCTION

The U.S. Fish and Wildlife Service (Service) and U.S. Army (Army) have negotiated a Memorandum of Agreement (MOA) under which much of the former Savanna Army Depot (Depot) in Northwestern Illinois will become Lost Mound National Wildlife Refuge (Lost Mound Refuge). The area is notable for its immense grasslands (4000 acres) and bottomland forest (5000 acres) habitats. Lost Mound Refuge supports endangered Higginsii Pearly Mussel (Lampsilis higginsii) and the threatened Bald Eagle (Haliaeetus leucocephalus). The Service has negotiated a Cooperative Agreement with the Illinois Department of Natural Resources (IDNR) for joint management of the area.

This Environmental Assessment (EA) has been developed by the Service in compliance with agency decision-making requirements of the National Environmental Policy Act of 1969, as amended.

I. PURPOSE AND NEED FOR ACTION

Purpose: The purpose of the proposed action is to preserve, restore, and manage 9,111 acres of high quality wildlife habitat along the Upper Mississippi River in Illinois at no acquisition cost to the Service. The goal of the Lost Mound Refuge is to manage for migratory birds.

Need for Action: The 4,000 acres of native sand prairies and sand savanna's at the former Savanna Army Depot are some of the last remaining prairies of their kind in Illinois and possibly the entire Mississippi River watershed. The area is also notable for its extensive 5000 acre bottomland forest. These uplands and wetlands provide habitat for 2 federally-listed threatened and endangered species and 47 State listed species. These valuable habitats could be significantly impacted or even lost altogether without action by the Service.

Background: The 1995 Base Realignment and Closure Commission (BRAC) made recommendations for the realignment and closure of the Depot and Congress approved the plan. The Depot operated from 1917 through 2000 and was initially used as a test firing range but was modified into a storage, disposal and manufacturing facility for munitions and explosives. The Depot is located on 13,062 acres of land in Northwestern Illinois along the Mississippi River. Through the disposal process the Service could acquire 9111 acres. The value of this area for threatened, endangered or sensitive species and habitats has only partially been identified. The IDNR was provided limited access in 1978 to manage natural resources and begin research. The Service and IDNR believe the bottomland forest and sand savanna/prairie habitats in this area contain significant floral and faunal resources of value to the State and Region. However, the quality of these habitats for Regional and State priority fish, wildlife and plant species has never been assessed. A complete survey of these natural assets is essential for future conservation management.

Approximately 3,300 acres in the southern portion of the former Depot is being developed by private interests. The Jo-Carroll Depot Local Redevelopment Authority (LRA) is the agency responsible for transfer of former Depot land to a private interest. Figure 1 depicts the future distribution of ownership and management rights on the former Depot. Other stakeholders receiving land management privileges include The State of Illinois and the U.S. Army Corps of Engineers.

II. THE ALTERNATIVES

The Department of the Army's Final Environmental Impact Statement for Disposal and Reuse of Savanna Army Depot Activity, Savanna, Illinois (FEIS) published in 1997 identified and compared several general reuse alternatives. The Service is adopting the preferred alternative identified in the FEIS. The FEIS extensively examines the environmental and socio-economic consequences of reuse of the former Depot as a wildlife refuge. However, the FEIS does not provide much information on potential recreational uses and public access to the future refuge. The authors of this EA view the public access issue as a key consideration for this EA. The No Action alternative of no Service involvement is also considered.

Alternatives Considered but Eliminated from Further Study.

Several management alternatives will not be evaluated in this EA because they were addressed in the Depot FEIS. The alternatives included the Army's No Action Alternative for redevelopment and the Alternative to Dispose Unencumbered. These alternatives were ruled out from further study because of the Army's exhaustive investigation for the Depot FEIS. Biological and cultural resources and other environmental parameters are described in great detail.

Because the Depot has been identified as a superfund site and placed on the National Priorities List, and also due to safety concerns over unexploded ordnance, land will not be transferred without encumbrances. The Service will not accept land in fee title if it contains unexploded ordnance or other environmental contaminants. Land will only be accepted in fee title once it is cleared of unexploded ordnance and determined clean and suitable for transfer by the Base Closure and Transfer Team. Some land may not be approved for fee title transfer by the team due to an unacceptable level of financial and public safety liability for the Service. Such lands will be managed under a MOA between the Service and Army. A Level 2 pre-acquisition contaminants survey completed for the Service details this issue.

Alternative A. No Action
The Lost Mound Refuge would not be established under the no action alternative. The Army would retain land and re-appropriate as necessary to remove land from its property inventory.

Figure 1

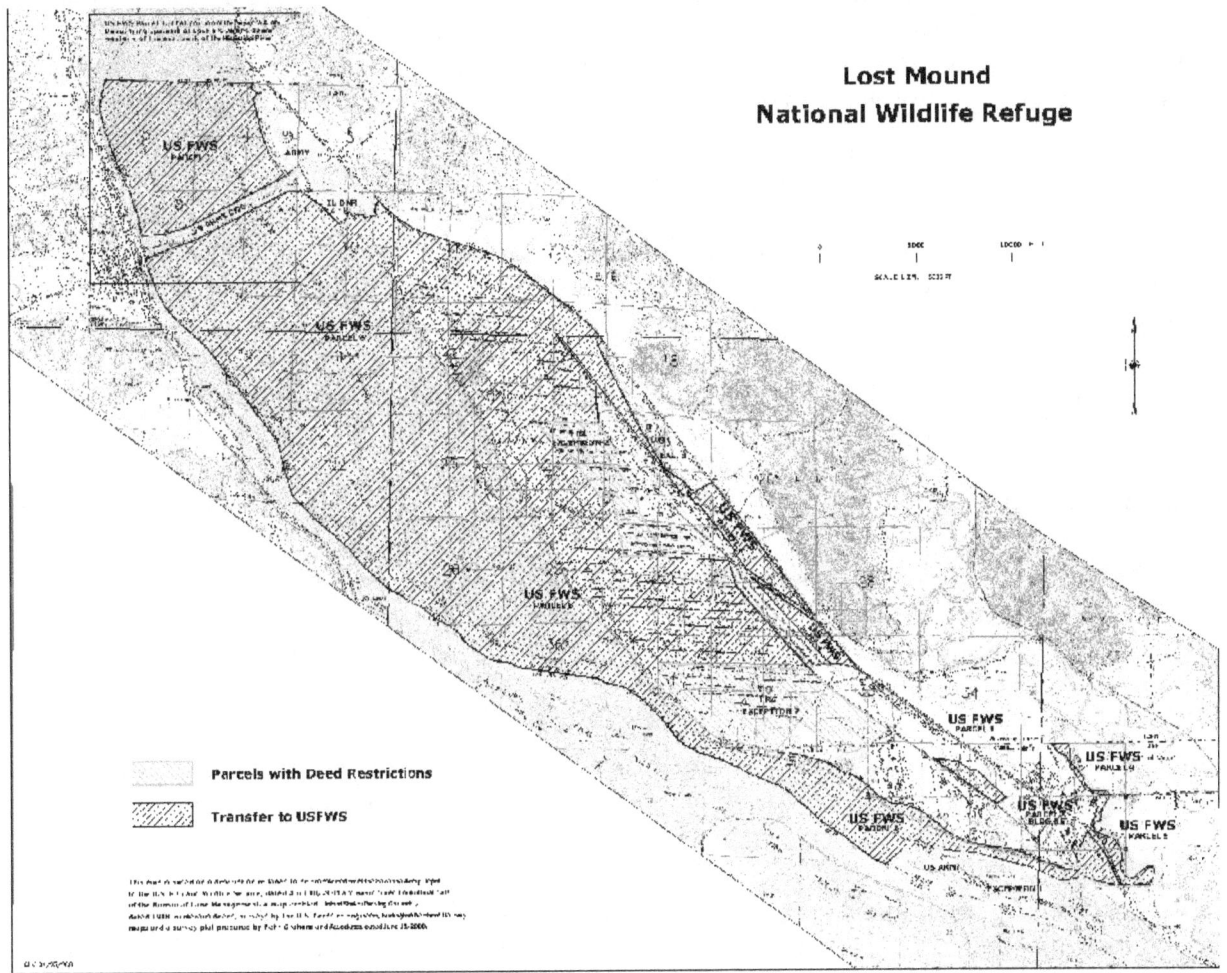

Lost Mound
National Wildlife Refuge

Alternative B. Refuge Establishment / No Public Use
The Service would establish the 9,111 acre Lost Mound Refuge but no public access would be allowed. The Lost Mound Refuge would not be open to the general public except in cases of emergency wildlife management actions (i.e. deer hunts for population control). The area would be managed solely as a protected wildlife sanctuary with access only for refuge administration.

Alternative C. Refuge Establishment / Limited Public Access (Preferred Alternative)
The Service would establish the Lost Mound Refuge and allow for limited public access. Placing limits on public access would give refuge staff the opportunity to manage endangered species and critical migratory bird habitat while still providing safe wildlife-dependent recreational use. Boat access to the backwater channels can be limited to reduce disturbance to eagle nests or the great blue heron rookery. The Lost Mound Refuge would allow public use and access on the uplands as approved by the Refuge Manager. Restrictions would be required to protect the fragile native sand prairie /savanna habitat.

III. AFFECTED ENVIRONMENT

The former Depot contains the last remaining native sand savanna/prairies in the Midwest, a feature once common in Illinois. The loss of this habitat elsewhere due to development and farming has highlighted this area for protection. Mowing and cattle grazing on the uplands once provided fire protection for the Depot but also suppressed the native prairie. Details of the local physical, cultural and biological resources can be found in documents such as the Depot FEIS, a report entitled Expansion of the Upper Mississippi River Wildlife and Fish Refuge on the Savanna Army Depot (Clarion Associates, Inc 1997) and within the Draft Conceptual Management Plan (USFWS 1996) published as an appendix to the FEIS.

The native sand prairies and sand savannas at the proposed Lost Mound Refuge are some of the last remaining prairies of their kind in the State and possibly the entire Mississippi River watershed. Along with the two federally-listed threatened and endangered species there are 47 State-listed species. There are 4000 acres of native sand prairie/savanna and 5000 acres of bottomland forest that were once designated the Bellevue-Savanna National Forest by President Calvin Coolidge in 1926. The Lost Mound Refuge would protect a seven mile long sand dune along the river's edge that rises up to 60 feet above the Mississippi River. A survey of the mussels in and around the Lost Mound Refuge is currently underway. To date there have been 23 mussel species identified in the Apple River adjacent to the Lost Mound Refuge. There are four nesting pairs of bald eagles within the Lost Mound Refuge backwaters area. Winter bald eagle counts have been recorded as high as 400 along the shoreline and within the interior backwaters area. A great blue heron rookery is also located in the bottomlands.

IV. ENVIRONMENTAL CONSEQUENCES

The environmental, social and economic benefits of the Depot reuse and no action alternative are fully explored in the 1997 FEIS. However, specific impacts related to habitat, trust resources of the Service such as migratory birds, and new recreational opportunities for the public were not addressed in detail in that document. The following issues/concerns apply directly to the Service's mission and the action of creating a National Wildlife Refuge.
Effects common to all alternatives:

Reuse of Depot facilities: Under all alternatives, the Jo-Carroll Local Redevelopment Authority would continue to develop industrial and commercial areas on the former Depot (Figure 1). The infrastructure of the public utilities including sewer, water and power would be maintained and provide services to local businesses. Activities that occur on the commercial areas should have minimal impact on the environment of the proposed refuge.

Historic resources: Cultural and historical resources will be considered under each alternative. The U.S. Army and the Service are both federal agencies and subject to the same laws protecting historical sites. Section 106 of the National Historic Preservation Act of 1966 requires federal agencies to identify cultural resources on federal property, evaluate those resources for the National Register of Historic Places, estimate potential effects of federal actions, and identify mitigation measures. The Illinois State Historic Preservation Office has provided consultation through development of the FEIS and during the Depot reuse decision process.

Alternative A. No Action

Fish and Wildlife Habitats: Loss of sand savanna/prairie habitat through natural succession will occur without an active Wildlife Management Activities Plan (attachment to MOA). The Plan is currently approved by the Army. With no action, the army will retain ownership of the sand savanna/prairie and backwaters areas and allow habitat to follow the natural succession process.

Threatened and Endangered Species: Loss of important habitats for both Federal and State-listed threatened and endangered species could occur under the no action alternative. Bald eagle wintering concentrations could be disturbed if the bluff area is developed under a new Depot disposal scenario.

Migratory Birds: The significant sand savanna/prairie habitat loss under this alternative would impact nesting songbirds. Several sand savanna/prairie-dependent species require large tracts of grass cover for nesting success. The no action alternative could lead to the loss of this habitat and all neo-tropical migrant birds found here.

Recreation and Environmental Education: Recreational uses and environmental education will not be allowed under this alternative. Public use would remain in the control of the Army thus, with their limited staff and funding the public would not have access to this area. Public access would be prohibited due to the presence of unexploded ordnance, environmental contaminants, and other safety and law enforcement issues.

Socioeconomic Environment: Operation of the Depot ceased in March 2000. The economic impacts of the base closure have been realized in the intervening years. Due to unexploded ordnance, the Army would likely continue to manage the site in caretaker status. The no action alternative would likely result in little additional economic impact. Local businesses would not benefit from an increase in visitors to the former Depot.

Partnerships and Cooperative Relationships: No new Service partnerships would result from this alternative. The Service and the Army have partnered to allow the Service to manage natural resources. The Service and IDNR have been working together since 1995 under a preliminary Cooperative Agreement. These two relationships would end. The Service, IDNR and Army could negotiate a cooperative relationship for wildlife habitat management under a limited term agreement. However, future alternative Depot reuse options, and Service funding for off-refuge work, could limit this relationship.

Alternative B. Refuge Establishment / No Public Use

Fish and Wildlife Habitats: Existing wildlife habitats will be maintained, increased and restored under this alternative. The Service will pursue a MOA with the Army for the management of the 9111 acres. A Cooperative Agreement between the Service and IDNR will maintain the 4,000 acres of sand savanna/prairie and 5,000 acres of forested backwaters.

Threatened and Endangered Species: The federally endangered Higginsii Pearly Mussel and the threatened bald eagle will both benefit from this alternative. The 780 acre State of Illinois designated mussel sanctuary will be protected from future disturbance. Nesting and wintering concentrations of bald eagles will receive increase protections through Service management of the area. The sensitive sand prairie uplands, with more than 30 state-listed plant species, will also receive a slight increase in protection with no public access.

Migratory Birds: Refuge establishment would protect existing migratory bird diversity. Expanded forest and grassland habitat management actions should lead to an increase in breeding/nesting habitat. Bird species diversity would remain stable or increase. Active management and restoration will increase and improve migratory bird habitat.

Recreation and Environmental Education: No recreational uses and environmental education programs would be allowed onsite. The proposed visitor safety precautions (visitor training, gate closures, limited entry permit system) under the draft Public Access Plan would not be necessary under this alternative. These uses will remain in the control of the Army thus, with their limited staff, funding constraints, and the presence of unexploded ordnance, the public would not have access to this area.

Socioeconomic Environment: Same as Alternative A. Refuge establishment without public use would not allow for an increase in eco-tourism and spending within the local economy. However, the local economy would benefit from a slight increase in federal spending for refuge operations.

Partnerships and Cooperative Relationships: Partnership opportunities would be limited under this alternative. It would be difficult to attract the interest of local business, sporting and environmental groups without access to the refuge itself. The IDNR and a few national organizations and regional universities may be interested in assisting with wildlife research projects.

Alternative C. Refuge Establishment / Limited Public Use

Fish and Wildlife Habitats: Same as Alternative B, except the public will be given the opportunity to participate in limited hunting, fishing, environmental education, interpretation, viewing and photography programs. A few small sites throughout the new refuge could be impacted by facilitating public use. However, any future public use support facilities, including boat landings and parking areas will receive specific environmental review.

Threatened and Endangered Species: Same as Alternative B for federally-listed species. Some loss of state-listed plant species and habitat is possible with limited public use. However, use of the uplands will be limited to established trails and roads. The IDNR will also be on-site to identify and mitigate potential disturbance of sensitive habitats.

Migratory Birds: Same as Alternative B.

Recreation and Environmental Education: The National Wildlife Refuge System Improvement Act of 1997 identified 6 priority wildlife-dependent public uses that may occur on a refuge if determined to be compatible with the mission of the National Wildlife Refuge System and the purposes of the refuge. Wildlife dependent public uses are defined as hunting, fishing, wildlife observation, wildlife photography, environmental education, and interpretation. All 6 priority public uses have previously occurred on the Depot through the Depot Sportsmen's Club. This Club permitted only Federal employees, military personnel and their guests access and participation. Wildlife-dependent recreational opportunities will increase under this alternative. The Lost Mound Refuge will continue wildlife dependent public uses administered with a limited entry, permitted, or guided system as outlined in the draft Public Access Plan (USFWS 2001, in prep.).

The Service's mandate for environmental education and interpretation will lead to new opportunities for local area schools and residents. Guided interpretive tours are proposed within the draft Public Access Plan. The existing road network, future trails system, and the diversity of habitats and species will make the Lost Mound Refuge a quality location for educational purposes.

Socioeconomic Environment: The number of visitors attracted to Lost Mound Refuge will increase with each passing year. The report "Maximizing the Economic Benefits of the Expansion of the Upper Mississippi River Wildlife and Fish Refuge on the Savanna Army Depot" (Clarion 1997) provides an investigation into the impact a refuge has on the local economy. The Clarion Report provides information about how wildlife observation in general provides recreation as well as a source of income for surrounding communities. Local sporting goods stores, gas stations and hotels may be among the businesses to benefit from the new refuge.

Partnerships and Cooperative Relationships: The close working relationship with the IDNR and U.S. Army Corp Of Engineers would continue under this alternative. Local sporting groups such as hunting and fishing clubs are also likely supporters of refuge activities. Many national wildlife refuges have sponsor organizations or "Friends" groups. These groups provide a ready pool of volunteers, community contacts and they also seek monetary grants for projects on a refuge from private and public sources. Establishment of the Lost Mound Refuge may lead to the formation of a Friends group.

V. REFERENCES, CONSULTATION AND COORDINATION

Clarion Associates, Inc. 1997. Maximizing the Economic Benefits of the Expansion of the Upper Mississippi River Wildlife and Fish Refuge on the Savanna Army Depot.

Gosse, Jeff. USFWS. Minneapolis, Minnesota. Personal Communication.

Robb, Joseph R. USFWS. Madison, Indiana. Personal Communication.

Sandusky, M. C. 1997. Final Environmental Impact Statement for BRAC 95 Disposal and Reuse of the Savanna Army Depot Activity, Savanna, Illinois. U.S. Army Materiel Command, Alexandria, Virginia.

U.S. Fish and Wildlife Service. 1997. Conceptual Management Plan for the Savanna Army Depot Wildlife Management Unit, Savanna, Illinois.

Prepared by:

Alan G. Anderson, Refuge Operations Specialist, Savanna District, Upper Mississippi River National Wildlife and Fish Refuge, Savanna, Illinois.

Gary E. Muehlenhardt, Branch of Ascertainment and Planning, U.S. Fish and Wildlife Service, Minneapolis, Minnesota.

Lost Mound National Wildlife Refuge
Savanna, Illinois

INTERIM COMPREHENSIVE CONSERVATION PLAN

U.S. Department of the Interior
Fish and Wildlife Service

3159 Crim Drive
Savanna, Illinois 61074
September 2001

INTERIM COMPREHENSIVE CONSERVATION PLAN
LOST MOUND NATIONAL WILDLIFE REFUGE

CONTENTS

INTRODUCTION

The Savanna Army Depot (Depot) is a 13,062 acre military installation that was closed in March 2000 by the Base Realignment and Closure (BRAC) Commission under Public Laws 100-526 and 101-510. Approximately 9,111 acres of the former Depot are proposed to be transferred to the U.S. Fish and Wildlife Service (Service) for operation as the Lost Mound National Wildlife Refuge (Lost Mound Refuge). The proposed refuge will include about 5,000 acres of bottomlands and about 4,000 acres of uplands. The Illinois Department of Natural Resources (IDNR) will enter into a cooperative agreement with the Service to jointly manage the refuge. The primary objective of the proposed Refuge is to provide migratory bird habitat and the continued conservation of wetlands and prairie habitat for the benefit of all wildlife species and wildlife-dependent public use.

This Interim Comprehensive Conservation Plan for the proposed Lost Mound Refuge presents a general outline on how the refuge will be operated and managed by the Service and IDNR until such time as a full Comprehensive Conservation Plan can be completed. Both agencies are included in this planning document to facilitate coordination of management efforts. As an interim plan, it does not provide extensive detail nor pinpoint exactly where facilities would be, or show where public use would be allowed. This plan includes a general discussion of biological needs relative to Federal trust resource responsibilities within that portion of the Upper Mississippi River/Tallgrass Prairie Ecosystem found in Illinois and the management actions required to meet those specific biological needs. It is not intended to cover in detail the development or implementation of specific programs for administration, public recreational use, or management of these public lands. Specific access sites and activities would be determined through future planning in compliance with the National Environmental Policy Act (NEPA). However, this plan should answer those questions commonly posed by neighbors and the general public during the planning and public involvement process which is now beginning with respect to establishment of Lost Mound Refuge.

There are three additional agencies that will acquire a primary interest in the former Depot. Coordination with each of these partners will be required to cooperatively manage the former Depot complex. The Service and IDNR will enter into cooperative agreement to jointly manage the refuge. The U.S. Army Corps of Engineers (COE) has requested 460 acres to include the 183 acre Apple River Island and 277 acres to expand the Blanding's Landing recreation area. The Local Redevelopment Authority (LRA) has already received 3,224 acres for economic development purposes which may include light and heavy industry.

Savanna Army Depot was purchased by the U.S. Army in 1917 and was used as a proof and test facility for artillery guns and howitzers. Operations expanded with the addition of ordnance storage facilities and loading and renovating shells and bombs. In 1972, ammunition maintenance and supply operations were reduced. The Deport mission prior to closure was the receipt, storage, issue, and demilitarization of conventional ammunition and general supplies. The U.S. Army Defense Ammunition

Center and School was located on the former Depot. The former Depot remains closed to general public access due to enforcement and environmental contaminant concerns. The former Depot was placed on the National Priorities List (Superfund) for clean-up in 1989 by the U.S. Environmental Protection Agency.

The Service is the primary Federal agency responsible for conserving, protecting, and enhancing the Nation's fish and wildlife resources and their habitats. The Service shares this responsibility with other Federal, State, tribal, local, and private entities; however, the Service has specific trustee responsibilities for migratory birds, endangered species, inter-jurisdictional fish, certain marine mammals, and lands and waters administered by the Service for the management and protection of these resources.

The Service operates over 530 national wildlife refuges nationwide, waterfowl production areas in ten states, and 51 coordination areas in 19 states, covering more than 92 million acres. These areas comprise the National Wildlife Refuge System, the world's largest collection of lands specifically managed for fish and wildlife. Approximately 76 million acres of these lands are in Alaska, with the remaining 17 million acres spread across the other 49 states and several Territories. There are 7 national wildlife refuges in Illinois. The Savanna District presently manages over 52,000 acres stretching 90 miles along the Mississippi River from Rock Island, Illinois to Dubuque, Iowa. The Lost Mound Refuge is located within this area and will complement ongoing management programs.

GOALS OF THE NATIONAL WILDLIFE REFUGE SYSTEM

*To preserve, restore, and enhance in their natural ecosystems (when practicable) all species of animals and plants that are endangered or threatened with becoming endangered.

*To perpetuate the migratory bird resource.

*To preserve a natural diversity and abundance of fauna and flora on refuge lands.

*To provide an understanding and appreciation of fish and wildlife ecology and man's role in his environment, and to provide refuge visitors with high quality, safe, wholesome, and enjoyable recreational experiences oriented toward wildlife to the extent these activities are compatible with the purposes for which the refuge was established.

REFUGE ADMINISTRATION

The proposed Lost Mound Refuge would become part of the National Wildlife Refuge System. Lost Mound staff would administer 9111 acres of bottomland and upland habitat with IDNR providing joint management through a cooperative agreement. During the last several years, a permanent Refuge Operations Specialist has been assigned to represent the Service's interests on the former Depot. Temporary employees are hired during the field season when funding permits, and could include biological aides, laborers, interns, and personnel through the Youth Conservation Corps, Job Training Partnership Act, and other programs for high school and college students.

The annual budget for the Lost Mound Refuge is yet to be determined. Funding for Lost Mound Refuge will be requested in future budgets. The IDNR will enter a Cooperative Agreement to jointly manage the Lost Mound Refuge. There is currently a staff of three IDNR personnel at Lost Mound Refuge. Existing facilities at the former Depot are being used and no new facilities are currently proposed. IDNR and the Service have co-occupied office space for the past three years. This has improved coordination of the two programs and provides a central location for the public to make contact with these management agencies.

ENVIRONMENTAL CONTAMINATION, HEALTH, AND SAFETY ISSUES

Savanna Army Depot was placed on the National Priorities List for Superfund cleanup in 1989. Approximately $320 million may be budgeted during the next 20 years for contaminants removal. Presently 69 environmental sites may require cleanup. Some of these contaminants include solvent, petroleum, lead, cadmium, and mercury. TNT contamination has been confirmed to have reached the groundwater and has spread three-fourths of a mile westward toward the Mississippi River. It is reported that 90% of the Depot has the potential to contain some unexploded ordnance to include 155 mm and 75 mm howitzers, mortars, grenades, and small arms ammunition.

These environmental contamination, health, and safety issues will be considered in identifying areas for public access to Lost Mound Refuge. The 9,111 acres that are proposed for addition to the National Wildlife Refuge System are to be used for conservation purposes, therefore the degree of clean-up will not be as strict as if housing or industry were proposed for the site. The U.S. Environmental Protection Agency (EPA), the Illinois Environmental Protection Agency (IEPA), and the Department of Army (DA) will ultimately determine when, and if, the contaminated sites are cleaned up to the extent that there are no environmental contamination, health, and safety concerns.

HABITAT MANAGEMENT

The transfer of the former Depot lands presents the Service and IDNR with a unique opportunity to continue to preserve an ecologically significant environment. Habitat management goals will focus on providing natural ecological systems. Habitat management techniques will be used to promote biological diversity within the ecological systems. Due to the military mission, a majority of habitat has remained in relatively good condition. The bottomlands and uplands are representative of historic environments containing large contiguous tracts of riverine and upland habitat.

WETLANDS: Approximately 5,000 acres of floodplain wetlands are found within the Lost Mound Refuge boundary. The wetlands include a mosaic of open water (lakes, ponds, Mississippi River), meandering backwater sloughs, floodplain forest, emergent marshes, and wet meadows. Lost Mound Refuge proposes to leave these wetlands in a natural condition and to manage these areas in a manner similar to other areas within the National Wildlife Refuge System. Burning and/or mowing could be used to remove undesirable vegetation or to control encroachment of woody vegetation. River habitat would be protected from livestock grazing and other intensive uses to reduce erosion and subsequent siltation of waters.

GRASSLANDS: Approximately 4,000 acres of uplands are found within the Lost Mound Refuge boundary. These areas consist primarily of sand prairie associations, but also includes an oak-ash savanna association. There are 488 buildings scattered throughout the grasslands. The Service has requested deed restrictions, including a reversionary clause, on 922 additional acres in the LRA designated area. The deed restrictions prohibit ground disturbance and permit access for research and management.

Grasslands would be managed to promote migratory birds, native vegetation, species diversity, and endangered species conservation. Areas of existing native prairie would be managed to retard encroaching shrubs, trees, and non-native grasses. Management techniques would include burning, limited grazing, mechanical, biological, and chemical treatment. Areas of non-native grasslands would be restored to native plants by seeding and/or transplanting. The feasibility of developing a plant nursery, as suggested by the LRA, will be examined by the IDNR. Management of the wetlands and the grasslands will contribute to meeting objectives of the Upper Mississippi River/Tallgrass Prairie Ecosystem.

FORESTS: Approximately 6,470 acres of forest are found within the former Depot and includes 4,743 acres of bottomland forest and 1,727 acres of upland forest. Forest management practices on the refuge would include burning, harvesting, seedling planting, or habitat manipulation depending on the particular objective of each area. The feasibility of developing a tree seed orchard will be examined by IDNR.

BIOLOGICAL MONITORING

The proposed Lost Mound Refuge contains diverse biological communities that support 228 species of fish and wildlife and 102 species of plants. There are 47 State listed and two Federally listed threatened and endangered species present. Important biological considerations include the presence of bald eagle nesting and roosting areas, heron rookeries, waterfowl concentration areas, grassland bird populations, fish and shellfish habitat, and extensive floodplain forest that is used by many species of neo-tropical migrant birds.

Since the primary purpose for establishing a national wildlife refuge is to conserve wildlife and habitat, extensive biological surveys are conducted throughout the year to identify animal and plant population trends. This information is the basis for refuge management decisions. A variety of wildlife surveys will be conducted to identify population densities and habitat use areas. Habitat surveys would include forest, wetland, and grassland inventories to document species diversity and densities.

Biological surveys would be conducted as a cooperative effort between IDNR and the Service. College, university, and other agencies would be encouraged to conduct research and population studies on plant and wildlife species.

The northern portion (approximately 850 acres) of the former Depot is presently identified in State of Illinois regulations as a mussel sanctuary and does not allow the commercial harvest of mussels. The Service will pursue mussel population investigations to determine the importance that this sanctuary provides as well as other open water areas within the Refuge. Native mussel populations are threatened within the Mississippi River system due to several factors that include zebra mussel invasion, pollution, and sedimentation.

PUBLIC ACCESS

Providing public access to IDNR and the Service managed lands will be important in keeping with the goal of the National Wildlife Refuge System. Lost Mound Refuge would provide a unique opportunity for outdoor enthusiasts to enjoy these public lands. The environmental contamination, health, and safety issues previously mentioned could restrict public access in certain areas.

Access to Lost Mound Refuge will need to be coordinated between the four partners (LRA, COE, IDNR, USFWS) due to the individual designated areas of use. The former Depot extends thirteen miles and includes over 100 miles of interior roads. Presently there is only one entrance road open. There are other access roads into the former Depot, but due to security requirements, these roads are closed. The present entrance road is located on proposed LRA lands. The Service has requested an easement for access to the entrance road as well as to other interior roads.

Geographically, the LRA area would be located at the southern end of the Depot and extend along the eastern boundary for approximately two miles. The Service land would extend along the northeastern boundary for about 10 miles. The IDNR designated lands extend along the east within the 10 miles identified for the Service. The COE parcels would extend along one mile of the northern end of the former Depot and the along the southern tip (Apple River Island).

The number of public entrances to the Service and IDNR lands would be limited for several reasons. The high speed rail crossings make additional entrances cost prohibitive and multiple entrances compound visitor use control, resource abuse, and increase manpower costs that could be used for resource management. An internal circulation route will be developed in coordination with all partners on the the former Depot complex to determine public vehicular access routes. The needs of persons with disabilities will be considered during access planning for any refuge activity or facility.

The Service and IDNR will not have the resources to maintain the many miles of roads that are present within the proposed Lost Mound Refuge. Primary routes of travel for public access will be designated and the remainder of the roads closed to vehicular traffic. Many of the interior roads provide access to the igloos and warehouses, which will not be opened to general public vehicular access. Foot access into these areas would be allowed for hikers, birdwatchers, photographers, and others. Signs and leaflets would clearly indicate the open and closed areas of the refuge.

Some habitat areas may become seasonally restricted sanctuary areas. These may include areas containing eagle nests and/or eagle roosts, heron rookeries, concentration areas for waterfowl, and areas where threatened and endangered plants are found.

PUBLIC RECREATIONAL ACTIVITIES AND MANAGEMENT

Wildlife dependent public use is encouraged on refuges as long as it is compatible with the primary purpose of the area. The Depot managed hunting, fishing and trapping programs for Depot employees, retirees, active and retired military personnel, and their guests prior to closure in March 2000. The Service and IDNR propose to offer these recreational activities to the general public, as well as add new programs.

Public recreational activities would be varied and could include both consumptive and non-consumptive uses. Actual uses will be identified through community involvement, public meetings, and planning efforts of a Citizen's Advisory Committee. General public use regulations, based on the National Wildlife Refuge System Act, are shown in Table 1.

Table 1. General Refuge Regulations

    *Public entry is permitted year round in those areas shown in the Refuge leaflet and marked by appropriate signs.

    *Vehicles are allowed only on main roads and trails where gates are open.

    *Use of the Refuge is limited to daylight hours only. No overnight parking is allowed.

    *Possessing or discharging firearms is prohibited except during established hunting seasons in areas open to hunting.

    *Disturbing or collecting any plant or animal is prohibited except under special use permit. Berry, nut, and mushroom picking are allowed in designated areas.

    *No person may search for, disturb, or remove from the Refuge any Native American artifact or other historical object, including military items.

    *Entering or remaining on the Refuge while under the influence of alcohol or other drugs is prohibited.

    *Dogs and other pets must be kept under control at all times.

The Lost Mound Refuge will offer many public recreational activities. It is anticipated that the following public use activities would be allowed at the proposed refuge.

HUNTING and TRAPPING: Hunting of waterfowl, small game, turkey, and white-tail deer would be permitted in some refuge areas in accordance with State regulations. These areas were once open to only military personnel and guests. Areas will be opened for public hunting dependent on the outcome of future management planning conducted with public input.

FISHING: Sport fishing would be permitted in accordance with State regulations. This area was once restricted to only military personnel and guests, it will now be open to the general public. Commercial fishing could be allowed under a Special Use Permit issued by the Refuge Manager.

BOATING, HIKING, CROSS-COUNTRY SKIING, AND OTHER USES: Many wildlife and wildlands oriented activities would be encouraged including hiking, bike riding, photography, cross-country skiing, canoeing, and wildlife observation. A designated hiking, bike riding, and skiing trail system is planned to be established. A self-guided auto tour route covering several miles would be established. Boating and canoeing would be permitted.

Service policy is that camping is only permitted on refuges where no other alternatives are available. The Service will not maintain the developed campground area located adjacent to the Coast Guard landing boat launch. Presently there are 16 known campgrounds providing over 1,000 campsites within 30 miles of Savanna. These areas provide ample opportunity for camper trailer enthusiasts. The Service will maintain the Coast Guard landing boat ramp. The ramp may need to be upgraded to handle perceived use.

ENVIRONMENTAL EDUCATION AND INTERPRETATION: Environmental education and interpretation programs would be designed to enhance the visitor's understanding of natural resource management programs and ecological concepts. Lost Mound Refuge would serve as an important "outdoor classroom" for area school districts. Teacher workshops would be offered to provide ongoing environmental education programs. Visitor facilities would be planned with the needs of students and teachers in mind. Interpretive programs would focus on self-guiding facilities such as auto tour routes, signed trails, leaflets, and interpretive signs located near interesting features. A visitor center would be set up within one of the existing buildings and contain an auditorium for slide and film presentations, exhibits, a classroom/meeting room, and possibly a bookstore offering natural resource materials to the public.

LAW ENFORCEMENT: Enforcement of State and Federal laws on national wildlife refuges is important to safeguard resources and to protect and manage visitors. The Service intends to seek concurrent jurisdiction from the State of Illinois. Refuge Officers would work closely with IDNR Conservation Officers and local enforcement personnel.

FACILITIES MANAGEMENT

The Service will receive a total of 394 buildings including 359 igloos, 30 warehouses, four administration buildings, 12 miles of fencing, eight miles rail line, 51 miles of roads, two bridges, container loading pad, three large rail line loading docks, five loading platforms, and one office building. The igloos have concrete floors, walls, and ceilings with steel doors and earthen exteriors. The warehouses have concrete floors and tile walls with metal doors and shingled roofs. Some of the warehouses may be used for storage, but initially most of the igloos and warehouses will be left vacant. In the event that LRA finds suitable leasing for all of its warehouses and still needs additional storage areas for economic use, the Service has agreed with LRA to lease/rent these igloos and warehouses. If no other use can be identified for these buildings, as funds become available in future years, they may be removed.

The Service has requested deed restrictions and a reversionary clause on 788 acres within the LRA designated use-areas. The reversionary clause requests that this area revert to the Service should the LRA not find a viable economic use for these areas within 20 years from the date it is available for economic use. Deed restrictions include no ground disturbance and access for research and management.

There are over 50 miles of railroad tracks on the former Depot. The Service would acquire several miles of these tracks. The igloos and warehouses have a loop system of rail lines with loading docks and loading platforms. This system will be kept intact until the River Port Rail lease runs out in March 2004. These lines are an inappropriate use and will be removed as funds become available. One office building will be transferred in fee title to Lost Mound Refuge.

The boundary of all Refuge lands would be posted with national wildlife refuge signs at regular intervals to identify to the public where the refuge boundary is. Fencing or other types of barriers may be constructed to control grazing or to control off-road vehicle use which can damage sensitive habitat, such as the upland sand prairie areas. Interpretive signs and kiosks would be placed throughout Lost Mound Refuge to inform the public of refuge regulations.

The Service will cooperate with LRA, COE, IDNR, State, County, and township officials in the maintenance of roads that cross Lost Mound Refuge. Roadside mowing within the refuge would be completed in accordance with State and local laws.

FIRE MANAGEMENT

It is the policy of the Service and IDNR to use fire when it is the most appropriate management tool for reaching habitat objectives. For example, a prescribed fire within the sand prairie uplands can serve to maintain the prairie area at the desired successional stage. Wildfires, however, would be aggressively suppressed unless natural fires are a part of the approved fire management plan. The use of prescribed fire will be dependent upon an approved plan and areas being cleared of explosives and or hazardous materials that would create a health and safety issue if fire were used.

IDNR and the Service have staffs trained in fire management and an array of equipment for fire suppression. To supplement these capabilities, cooperative agreements and contracts with State agencies and community fire departments would be put together to tap local firefighting expertise. This is especially important for structural fires since local fire departments have the special training and experience required for this type of fire fighting.

CROP DEPREDATIONS AND PEST CONTROL

The Service and IDNR would provide technical advice to landowners surrounding Lost Mound Refuge if crop losses occur from migratory birds, deer, or other refuge wildlife. The U.S. Department of Agriculture has an Animal Damage Control Division that can provide more direct assistance. It is Service policy to control those weeds listed as noxious by the State. This control would emphasize non-chemical methods.

ENVIRONMENTAL CONTAMINATION, HEALTH, AND SAFETY CONCERNS

A large portion of the former Depot has the potential to contain unexploded ordinance. In addition, 69 environmental sites may require cleanup. It is imperative that liability for the future cleanup of known as well as unknown environmental contaminant areas be the responsibility of the Department of Army. The Service has no plans to construct any buildings outside areas cleared of unexploded ordinance by the Army, however, some refuge activities as well as public use activities will require subsurface disturbance. These activities include: the placement of boundary posts, sign posts, kiosks; scenic overlook construction; and trapper stakes and/or hunting blind supports driven into the ground. The transfer of property should identify: 1) the Department of Army is responsible for any future hazards from unexploded ordinance and environmental contamination and, 2) the Department of Army should pay for the cost of sweeping an area if it is identified for construction at a later date.

RAILROAD LINES AND UTILITY INFRASTRUCTURE

The Burlington Northern Railroad Company has a major railroad line located along the east edge of the former Depot and traveling the entire length. Trains pass through on an hourly basis at speeds reaching 50 miles per hour. Only one railroad crossing has warning lights. The Service must consider the liability for public access at several railroad crossings. The purchase, installation, and maintenance of railroad crossing signals would be an expensive proposition.

There are many miles of overhead electrical power lines and underground telephone cables. However, all of these utilities are under a right-of-way easement to be maintained by the utility company.

STAFF, MATERIALS, AND EQUIPMENT NEEDS

Lost Mound Refuge will provide a unique opportunity for the Service to acquire an area of high environmental value. This natural area will require some habitat enhancement and maintenance. In addition, there will be many roads to close off (presumably with gates) and miles of roads to maintain.

The proposed Lost Mound Refuge presently has one permanent staff member assigned from the Savanna District (District) of the Upper Mississippi River National Wildlife and Fish Refuge. The IDNR has five staff onsite. District work loads are heavy and some refuge management activities are not being accomplished. It will be necessary to prioritize the existing work load, cut back existing programs, and use outside help, if the opportunities at the former Depot are to be implemented.

The closure of the Depot has generated much public interest because now people will be given the opportunity to see and do things that could not be allowed previously. The ultimate success of Lost Mound Refuge will be dependent upon how much time, effort, and dollars the Service can put into this new program. There are many opportunities available at Lost Mound Refuge to include public recreation, environmental education, and outreach programs. However, it will require increased funding or some significant sacrifices of other Service programs to operate above the "caretaker" status. The degree of success of the resource and facility management of Lost Mound Refuge will depend to a large degree upon additional funding, partnerships with the IDNR, LRA, COE, and others, and volunteer assistance and support from private individuals and groups.

INTERIM COMPATIBILITY DETERMINATION

Use(s): All Wildlife-dependent Recreational Uses

Refuge Name: Lost Mound National Wildlife Refuge

Establishing and Acquisition Authorities: The proposed Lost Mound National Wildlife Refuge (Refuge) will be created from lands currently within the Savanna Army Depot. Lands will be transferred from the jurisdiction of United States Army through a combination of fee-title land transfers and overlay management responsibilities under a Memorandum of Agreement. The Refuge will be established by the statutory authority of two specific acts:

> 1) The Fish and Wildlife Act of 1956 [16 USC 742a-742j] as amended authorizes the Secretary of the Interior to acquire interests in property "...for the development, advancement, management, conservation, and protection of fish and wildlife resources..."

> 2) The Endangered Species Act authorizes the Secretary of Interior to acquire interests in lands "to conserve fish, wildlife, and plants, including those which are listed as endangered or threatened..." [16 USC 1534].

Refuge Purpose: Lost Mound Refuge will be established for migratory birds and development, advancement, management, conservation, and protection of fish and wildlife resources, including those which are listed as endangered or threatened. The mission of Lost Mound Refuge derives from these two purposes: "to preserve, conserve and research biodiversity, to restore and maintain the highest quality biological resources and provide wildlife-dependent public use to the benefit of present and future generations of Americans."

National Wildlife Refuge System Mission: The Mission is to administer a national network of lands and waters for the conservation, management, and where appropriate, restoration of the fish, wildlife, and plant resources and their habitats within the United States for the benefit of present and future generations of Americans.

Description of Use: This Compatibility Determination will review priority wildlife-dependent recreational uses, as defined by the National Wildlife Refuge System Improvement Act of 1997 (Act), to include hunting, fishing, environmental education, interpretation, wildlife observation and photography. Section 6(3)(A)(ii) of the Act states: "On lands added to the System after March 25, 1996, the Secretary shall identify, prior to acquisition, withdrawal, transfer, reclassification, or donation of any such lands, existing compatible wildlife-dependent recreational uses that the Secretary determines shall be permitted to continue on an interim basis pending completion of the comprehensive conservation plan for the refuge."

All 6 priority public uses have previously occurred on the Savanna Army Depot through the Depot Sportsmen's Club. This club permitted only Federal employees, military personnel and their guests access and participation. The club was dissolved when the Savanna Army Depot was closed in March 2000. The Service is proposing to administer a new public use program with a limited entry, permitted, or guided system as outlined in the draft Public Access Plan, currently in preparation.

The opportunities for high quality wildlife-dependent public use (hunting, fishing, environmental education, interpretation observation and photography) will allow the Lost Mound Refuge to achieve one of its three goals to the extent these activities are compatible with the mission of the Refuge.

Availability of Resources: Service funding/staffing to the proposed Lost Mound Refuge (Savanna Army Depot) is currently provided through the Savanna District of the Upper Mississippi River National Wildlife and Fish Refuge. If established, the Refuge will continue to share equipment and staff. In addition, the refuge may gain some revenue from commercial leases. Demand for public use will likely exceed the limits described in the draft Public Access Plan and will need to be regulated. However, costs to administer the public use program should only minimally exceed current expenses and receipts.

Anticipated Impacts of the Use(s):

(A.)   Direct Impact: The uses proposed will help to attain Lost Mound Refuge goals to increase opportunities for public uses and to protect, restore, and manage bottomland forest sand savanna/prairie habitat. Also, the increases in public use of Lost Mound Refuge will help develop an appreciation of the natural character of the area. Threatened and endangered species and their habitats will not be jeopardized because all traffic within recreational areas will be restricted to protect these resources. Habitats for the 47 state-listed threatened and endangered wildlife and plant species will be monitored by the Service and Illinois Department of Natural Resources staff to ensure a minimum of disturbance.

(B.)   Indirect Impact: Allowing these uses will help the Refuge to develop an appreciative and informed base of public support for Lost Mound Refuge programs, increase success of refuge habitat restoration activities (sand savanna/prairie restoration, and protecting bottomland forest habitat), and foster a cooperative relationship with adjacent landowners.

Public Review and Comment: This Interim Compatibility Determination will be published and distributed along with a Draft Environmental Assessment for establishment of the Lost Mound Refuge and an Interim Comprehensive Conservation Plan. The public will be invited to comment on all three documents during a 30-day review period.

Determination (check one below):

_____ **Use is Not Compatible**

__X__ **Use is Compatible With Following Stipulations**

Stipulations Necessary to Ensure Compatibility:

Vehicular traffic will only be allowed on designated roads of travel, thus reducing the impact recreational activities will have on sensitive habitat types.

Control of various wildlife populations, especially white-tailed deer, will enhance the ability of the refuge staff to conserve healthy communities of fish, wildlife, and plants necessary to fulfill Refuge purposes.

The proposed hunting and fishing areas, with applicable restrictions and maps, are discussed in a Natural Resources Management Activity Plan. Areas open to wildlife observation and photography, and environmental education and interpretation will be outlined in the draft Public Access Plan.

Justification: The proposed uses are compatible because they are within the establishing authority language, fulfill the intent of the Refuge Improvement Act of 1997 concerning wildlife-dependent public use, and there are no federal regulations prohibiting the uses. The uses do not jeopardize the fulfillment of any of Lost Mound Refuge's other primary goals.

Signature: Refuge Manager: _____
                                                (Signature and Date)

Concurrence: Regional Chief: _____
                                                (Signature and Date)

Mandatory 15-year Re-evaluation Date: _____

www.ingramcontent.com/pod-product-compliance
Lightning Source LLC
Chambersburg PA
CBHW081141280526
45787CB00007B/3178